LEGEND COCKTAILS

by

Murray Powell

GW00705955

R&R PUBLICATIONS MARKETING PTY LTD

This edition published by
R&R Publishing Pty. Ltd.
ABN 78 348 105 138
PO Box 1221 Fitzroy North VIC 3068
National toll free: 1 800 063 296
Email: info@randrpublications.com.au
Web: www.randrpublications.com.au

Publisher: Richard Carroll
Author: Murray Powell
Cover Design: Danielle Harlow
Typesetting: Sean McNamara
Photography: Warren Webb
Presentation: Murray Powell
Photography Assistance: Jon Carroll
Proofreading: Pamela Mawbey

The National Library of Australia
Cataloguing-in-Publication Data
Legend Cocktails.
Includes index.
ISBN: 1-74022-268-7

1. Cocktails. 2. Title: Legend Cocktails.

641.874

First Printed July 1996
Reprinted in August 2006

Computer Typeset in Nuptial Script, Gill Sans and Palatino
Printed in China

Table of Contents

LEGEND COCKTAILS

HOW TO HOST A COCKTAIL PARTY AT HOME

INTRODUCTION

Everyone has tried a lush cocktail and said "Mmmm, God that's unreal! It even beats a Scotch and Coke" (if that's what you drink).

Now here's the chance for you to get that same reaction right in your own home.

Take heed of my general advice and, above all, have a ball.

Murray Powell

GENERAL ADVICE

You're not supposed to know everything or have everything, but here's a list of things I suggest you consider:

- Do I have, or will I have to borrow, *a Blender and a Shaker?*
- Do I have the *glasses* already, do I know a discount store to get a couple of dozen cheaply, will I just hire some, or will I scam some off my friends?
- Send an official *invitation* because it adds to the anticipation of the party. On it you can note what they are required to bring, and that way they won't forget. Photocopy the invite in the back of the book or make your own.
- *Dress* to impress – extra smart casual is best
  Don't make it formal as people worry too much about clothes, and most guys don't want to hire a tux if they don't have one.
  Don't make it ultra casual as people tend to treat it as a beer swilling barby, and it will soon get out of control.
- Try to *avoid beer* – for the same reasons as above.
- The best idea for numbers is *20–40 people.*
  Less than 20 is not a real cocktail party.
  More than 40 makes it too much trouble and work for the host, and again it can easily get out of hand.
- You need approximately *2 glasses* per person but you can get away with less if you are willing to wash them more often. Generally, the more glasses the better. Ask a few friends, they may have some you can borrow. You can't have too many glasses.
- Tell everyone *what to bring,* but tell your closest friends last (they really won't mind). That way if someone drops out, and there's always one that does, your closest friends can get the dropouts' bottle and all is not lost. However, you are the final straw.
- Get the couples coming to *bring* an expensive bottle and some fruit or juice. Get your more wealthy friends to bring expensive bottles. Get your poorer friends to bring the cheaper bottles.
  Remember, the costs will mount up, especially if you are providing glasses, nibblies, ice, etc., so *you* shouldn't have to buy a bottle…but then again, if you are going to run out of a key ingredient early in the night…you just might.

- Males and Females – don't just invite all of one *sex* as you then lose the romantic overtones. Besides, it's always best if it's someone from the opposite sex who says "I'd like an Orgasm please!!!" (well, for most people anyway).
- Ideally, tell each person to bring *a bottle and some fruit,* for example:
  Cointreau and strawberries, or
  Bacardi and orange juice, or
  Kahlúa and cream
  It's not just alcohol that goes into cocktails, it's all the ingredients that make them taste the way they do.
- Don't forget or under estimate the ice. A rough estimate would be a normal bag per 5 people. Remember, ice melts, so keep it in an esky.
- Have a *clean hammer* or meat mallet handy to break up the ice that always seems to form into solid rocks.
- *Garnishes* – rockmelon, honeydew melon, pineapple, oranges, lemons, and strawberries. Chop, slice and stick them on the glass. Use your imagination or look at the picture and try to copy that. Try getting some umbrellas, and coloured toothpicks, as they always look impressive and don't cost much. Don't forget the straws and remember, a drink tastes twice as good in a well-dressed glass.
  As a rough guide:
  fruity cocktails – fruits, umbrellas & straws
  creamy cocktails – just a strawberry
  strong cocktails – just a slice of lemon
  Also, the first couple of cocktails per person should be garnished nicely, but as the night wears on…to hell with it. Everyone will be drinking and having fun regardless of the garnishes.
- *Prepare* everything well in advance. You should garnish some glasses before the guests arrive.
- *How much fruit* to get:
  1 punnet of strawberries for every 5 people
  1 tin of mango slices for every 5 people
  1 banana for every 5 people
  1 rockmelon for every 30 people
  1 honeydew melon for every 30 people
  1 pineapple for any number of people
- Keep a couple of *teatowels handy*. You can dry your hands on them and spills do happen. Don't get upset with the spiller, just get them to clean up any mess. A moist cloth nearby is also a good idea.

- **Note:** When layering a shot, *layer as listed:*

Baileys	top	add last
Midori	middle	add second
Kahlúa	bottom	pour first

  So, the bottom ingredient on the list goes in first, then the ingredient above that. The ingredient on the top of the list goes in last, into the top of the glass. Simple.
- Remove all unnecessary benchtop items from the kitchen. Microwaves, fruitbowls, etc. should be taken away. *Bench space* is important. The more, the better. Line all the alcohol up along the back of the benches. During the party, try to keep the bench reasonably clean so the bottoms of the glasses remain clean. Push the bottles back and wipe the areas with a cloth as required.
- Try to dedicate a *piece of bench space* for dirty glasses. Don't let people put dirty glasses in your clean working areas. This area should take about 20 normal glasses. (You may be able to use the top of the stove at some houses.)
- Throw all the *bottle caps into a jar* or glass when you open them. It just slows things down if you keep taking the cap off and putting the cap on. At the end of the night, you can work out which cap belongs on which bottle pretty easily.
- Try to have 2 people *making the cocktails.* You can always blame a stuff-up on "the other person" and besides, it's faster and more fun.
- A good bartender will always *try each new cocktail* before it goes out. Suck some through a straw or pour a capful into your "tasting" glass. After all, you don't want to be banished from your own party for serving a dud.
- Start the night with *a few party favourites,* such as a Mango Daiquiri, a Splice, a blended Orgasm, a Japanese Slipper and a Pina Colada.
- Expect a little *mess* at the end on the night, and a huge clean-up in the morning.
- *Theme parties* can be fun, but generally the cocktails will be enough.
- Try to keep everyone *out of the kitchen.* It won't take long otherwise, until you can't move and it gets really annoying.
- This book lives *in the kitchen,* don't let it wander.
- As the host, try to *stand out.* Wear something bright, or wear a vest and bow tie. Don't wear anything loose like a regular tie or unbuttoned shirt, it's a real nuisance.
- Get some willing person to *wash dirty glasses* for you. Your job is making wicked cocktails, and they won't

mind helping out. Don't use the dishwasher because glasses come out too hot. Wash creamy cocktail glasses out under hot water. Rinse all others under cold water. They'll be just as clean, but ready to use after a quick rub with a teatowel. Note, wipe off any lipstick with a teatowel.

- *Encourage people* to drink "softer" cocktails if they seem to be only having shots. Slow down the guys who want to drink only the strong cocktails because one drunken idiot can spoil a good party for everyone else. A couple of shots and a couple of regular cocktails makes for a great evening.

- It's usually best if some people don't drive home. Tell people when they RSVP that there is plenty of carpet space going cheap. They may like to bring a pillow and sleeping bag. Keep the local cab company phone number near the phone. Remember: don't drink and drive (you might spill some).

- If someone is having a birthday at the party, *buy them a copy* of this book. That way there will be one copy in the kitchen, and one copy for everyone else to read. That way they will stop pestering you for a look.

Chips, Dips, Nibblies, Nuts and Fairy Bread (see page 12)

THE ESSENTIALS

The following is a list of the essentials for a successful cocktail party. Some are used in numerous cocktails so you may need a couple of bottles.

ALCOHOL
Bacardi
Cointreau
Kahlúa
Baileys
Sambuca
Midori
Malibu
Vodka
Tequila

ADDITIVES & OTHERS
Blender & Shaker
Glasses
Ice
Sugar syrup
Lemon juice
Pineapple juice
Cream
Milk
Fruit
Can opener
Cocktail recipes

Don't forget the *music* but let somebody else worry about it. Chuck a few *ashtrays* outside for the smokers and have some nibblies lying around because people tend to eat and drink or smoke and drink.

TRICKS OF THE TRADE

- You can't buy *sugar syrup*. You make it. Boil 600ml of water and add sugar. Stir in sugar until no more sugar will dissolve. Sugar syrup is used in Daiquiris. Make it earlier in the day (as hot sugar syrup will heat the drink) then leave it in the fridge to cool.
- *An alternative to sugar syrup* is lime cordial – not green cordial – lime cordial. It has roughly the same level of sweetness as sugar syrup, and adds a citrus flavour to the cocktail. In drinks such as a Daiquiri you put in lemon juice anyway so the lime flavour won't matter. Actually, lime cordial can be used wherever sugar syrup is stated. If they do it in cocktail bars, why shouldn't you do it at home?
- When making the cocktails, you really *don't need nip pourers* or the like. It's more impressive to free-pour from a bottle than to s-l-o-w-l-y get the exact amount. Practise pouring 30ml into a shot glass or measuring cup until you can consistently pour in the range of 25-35ml. When you add all the other ingredients to the cocktail, 5ml here or there won't matter. Free-pourers can add that touch of class to the evening, and you can get cheap ones for about a dollar. They're not essential but look good.
- In this book you'll find the recipes use *parts* instead of nips or 30ml measures. The reason for this is that most of the time you will be making a blender full of cock- tail, and you may get 2, 3, or 4 full glasses from one blender. If you are making only one glassful, *try using 30ml = one part.* (The exception to this is for shots which would then be 10–10–10.)
- Obviously, if your making three Pina Coladas in the same blender, you're going to have to guess 90ml of Bacardi. So *just pour 30–30–30.* No problem.
- When pouring a layered drink into a shot glass, *don't bother about using a spoon.* It's probably quicker and eas- ier, and gives better results, if you just take your time and tilt the glass so it slides down the inside. If con- venient, get someone else to do them and do five at once – it's quicker that way.
- *Straws* only come in one size. For shallow drinks in tumblers or martini glasses, you really need a short straw. Just use a non-serrated knife to *cut them in half.* And put the rough end of the straw in the drink.
- For each of the non-alcoholic ingredients there is an *indication* of how much to put in. For less potent drinks

use less alcohol. For more potent drinks use more alcohol. But in general, *make the drink fit the glass.* If you follow the ingredients to the millilitre, you're not going to have fun. You're going to be too slow, and you're going to end up with either too much or not enough cocktail for the glass.

- You're there to have fun too! *Have a taste* to see if you've got it right, and add more of whatever you think is required to make it fit the glass.
- *Two blenders* are better than one – it's quicker and more convenient. Surely one of your closer friends has a blender you can borrow.
- *Grenadine* is a *very red/pink* colouring agent that gets added to various cocktails to enhance their colour. It is very easy to pour *too much.* To make sure you don't, you can either cut ⅓ of a wine cork out (long ways) and then jam it in the top, or punch a nail or knife through the cap. Either way, only a drop or two at a time should come out. You can always add more to a drink but you can't take it out.
- *Avoid using* passionfruit and kiwifruit because although they taste good, they leave little black bits in the cocktail which taste gritty. Also avoid watermelon as it has a thick skin, seeds throughout the melon, and does not taste good in cocktails.
- Chop the top off all strawberries, and *push strawberries* onto the rim of the glass. Don't cut them, they stay on better pushed, and take a lot less time to do. If you take the tops off the strawberries, you won't find "green bits" the next day when cleaning up, because people like to eat strawberries.
- *When making Daiquiris,* you can change the whole taste of them by adding milk or cream. Try it, you might like it.
- *Use tinned fruit* in cocktails, rather than fresh fruit, because it's normally softer and will blend to give a smoother cocktail. This does not apply to strawberries and bananas.
- When *using a Shaker,* half fill it with ice, 4 or 5 cubes should do.
- To *kick the party along,* send someone round with a tray of shots, just like a tray of fairy bread, only alcoholic.
- For a change, you may like to *blend instead of shake* the cocktails. This works best with creamy cocktails.
- *Stand your straws,* umbrellas and toothpicks up in appropriately sized glasses on the bench for easy access. It's a hassle to have to dig around in plastic bags for them.

GLASSES AND STUFF

GLASSES

- Try to get a selection of *3 or 4 types of glasses.* All one type is OK but a little boring. To compensate for only one type of glass I suggest you garnish more glasses and try to do some imaginative garnishing.
- Apart from the glasses you have hanging around home, try to get some highballs, martini glasses and lots of "cocktail" glasses. Have a *look at some of the photos* and you'll see the type of glasses I mean.
- The most important thing is to use glasses with a *sturdy base.* Wine glasses are not a particularly good idea as they topple over too easily.
- Large fancy *cocktail glasses* are great but you never have enough of them and people sometimes feel "ripped off" if their cocktail is in a smaller glass than their mates'. So don't go out of your way to get big ones.
- See if you can get a few *shot glasses* (the kind they have in nightclubs) from somewhere, it really makes the evening. Ask your friends to raid their parents' bars, you'd be surprised who has little glasses hidden away.
- *Don't use plastic cups.* They are light and spill easily. You can't put any sort of garnish on a plastic cup and it cheapens the party. Go for glasses.

CHIPS, DIPS, NIBBLIES, NUTS & FAIRY BREAD

- *Chips* – "Kettle chips hand cooked potato chips are the best" Get both "Chilli" and "Original Salted" because although Chilli will make you drink more, not everyone can handle them. Strong cornchips or crackers are also good because they don't break off in the dip.
- *Dips* – any dip will do, go to the supermarket or make your own.
- *Nibblies* – well, party pies and sausage rolls are always a winner at 11pm, other nibblies really depend on how much trouble you want to go to…remember though, they came for cocktails, not a feast.
- *Nuts* – cashews normally disappear before you can say "Long Slow Comfortable Screw Up Against A Wall"!!! Therefore mixed salted nuts are advised because they last longer and the salt makes people drink more.
- *Fairy bread* – you'd be surprised how many people say "Fairy bread!, I haven't had that in years!" and guaranteed, if it's good fairy bread with lots of 100s and 1,000s, there'll be none left in the morning (regardless of the average age of your guests).

WHAT IF I DON'T HAVE...

Bacardi:	Any white Rum, Vodka or Cointreau or a combo of both (for Daiquiris), if you get really desperate use a mixture of Gin and Tequila
Baileys:	Creme de Grand Marnier or Creme de Bananas or if you get desperate try Kahlúa and cream
Cointreau:	Grand Marnier or Triple Sec, and if really desperate try Brandy + OJ
Kahlúa:	Tia Maria or Baileys
Malibu:	Use coconut cream and Vodka or if an extreme emergency use Wipeout or Bombora
Midori:	Experiment with other fruit liqueurs like Mango, Banana or Strawberry, or if desperate, blend some honeydew melon and add Vodka
Sambuca:	Only in emergencies, Ouzo or Pernod
Tequila:	Vodka or Bacardi
Vodka:	Bacardi or Cointreau, or if you're desperate try Gin or Tequila or Schnapps (not much)
Any Colour:	Blue – Blue Curacao; Green – Creme de Menthe; Red – Grenadine; Yellow – Banana Liqueur or Advocaat
Anything Good Left:	Improvise and experiment. Use fruit and ice and the blender, raid tinned fruit from the cupboard, use milk and cream and ice cream, food dyes, Milo, choc topping – but *taste it before serving!*

AFTER DINNER MINT

1 part Baileys
1 part Creme de Menthe
1 part Kahlúa
(layer)

AMERICA'S CUP

2 parts Southern Comfort
1 part Bacardi
1 part Galliano
3 parts pineapple juice
3 parts orange juice
3 parts cream
(shake)

ANABOLIC STEROID

1 part Cointreau
1 part Midori
1 part Blue Curacao
(layer)

BETWEEN THE SHEETS

1 part Brandy
1 part Bacardi
1 part Cointreau
½ part lemon juice
(shake)

B-52

1 part Cointreau
1 part Baileys
1 part Kahlúa
(layer)
or
add 2 parts cream, ice & blend

BIZARRE

1 part Strawberry Liqueur
1 part Malibu
1 part Opal Nera
2 parts cream
(shake)

BLACK NIPPLE

1 part Baileys
1 part Opal Nera
(layer)

BLACK RUSSIAN

1 part Kahlúa
1 part Vodka
ice
(build)

for a weaker Black Russian
add 4 parts coke

for a White Russian
add milk instead of coke

BLACK WIDOW

1 part cream
1 part Opal Nera
1 part Strawberry Liqueur
(layer)

BLOW JOB

1 part Baileys
1 part Banana Liqueur
1 part Kahlúa
(layer)

BLUE HAWAIIAN

1 part Bacardi
1 part Blue Curacao
4 parts pineapple juice
1 part cream
ice
(blend)

BRAIN HAEMORRHAGE

4 drops of grenadine on top
⅕ part Baileys
⅖ parts Sambuca
⅖ parts Midori
(layer slowly)

BRANDY ALEXANDER

1 part Brandy
1 part Creme de Cacao
2 parts cream
(shake)
nutmeg on top

CARESSER

1 part Baileys
1 part Bacardi
4 parts milk
ice
(build)

CHEEKY GIRL

1 part Kahlúa
1 part Banana Liqueur
½ part Brandy
½ part Malibu
½ a banana
2 parts cream
ice
(blend)

CHEER

1 part Midori
1 part Gin
1 part lime cordial
lots of ice
(blend)
then add 6 parts lemonade

CHERRY RIPE

1 part Creme de Cacao
1 part Cherry Brandy or Cherry Advocaat
½ part Malibu
2 parts cream
(shake)

CHICKEN FOETUS

dash of Advocaat
dash of Cherry Advocaat
¼ part Baileys
¾ part Sambuca
(layer)

COFFEE BREAK

2 parts Tia Maria
1 part Malibu
4 parts milk
ice
(build)

COINTREAU AND LIME

1 nip Cointreau
¼ fresh lime or lemon, cut into pieces
crushed ice
(build)
Extract the lime juice in the glass by crushing,
fill with ice and add Cointreau.
Stir (a mini-pestle is best).

CUMFY ALEXANDER

1 part Southern Comfort
1 part Creme de Cacao
2 parts cream
(shake)

DAIQUIRIS

1 part Fruit Liqueur
1 part Bacardi
½ part lemon juice
½ part sugar syrup
fruit
ice
(blend)

DAIQUIRIS

Banana
Strawberry
Honeydew Melon
Rockmelon
Mango, Peach
Apricot, Pineapple
Kiwi fruit, Lychee
anything
If no Fruit Liqueur available
use double Bacardi

DEATH

1 part Tequila
1 part Opal Nera
(layer)

DIRTY DEVIL

1 part Strawberry Liqueur
1 part Kahlúa
(dash of) Malibu
strawberries
2 parts cream
ice
(blend)

FLAMING LAMBORGHINI

1 part Kahlúa
1 part Brandy
1 part Grand Marnier
1 part OP Rum on top (last)

light, suck thru a straw QUICKLY
then when almost gone
pour in a shot of
Blue Curacao or Creme de Menthe

FLUFFY DUCK

1 part Advocaat
1 part Cointreau
1 part cream
10 parts lemonade (add slowly)
(build & stir)

FREDDY FUDDPUCKER

1 part Tequila
½ part Galliano
6 parts orange juice
ice
(build)

FROOZE

1 part Cointreau
1 part Midori
1 part Malibu
2 parts milk
ice
(blend)

GOLDEN DREAM

1 part Cointreau
½ part Galliano
2 parts orange juice
1 part cream
(shake)

GRASSHOPPER

1 part Creme de Menthe
1 part Creme de Cacao
2 parts cream
(shake)

HARBOUR TUNNEL

1 part Kahlúa
1 part Creme de Cacao
1 part Baileys
4 parts milk
ice
(blend)
Milo on top

HARD ON

1 part Tequila
1 part Southern Comfort
1 part Kahlúa
(layer)

HARVEY WALLBANGER

1 part Galliano
1 part Vodka
6 parts Orange Juice
ice
(build)

HAWAIIAN HONEYMOON

1 part Bacardi
1 part Sambuca
2 parts orange juice
2 parts pineapple juice
½ part lemon juice
ice
(build)

HELLRAISER

1 parts Opal Nera
1 part Midori
1 part Strawberry Liqueur
(layer)

HOT DREAM

1 part Cointreau
1 part Galliano
2 parts pineapple juice
1 part cream
ice
(blend)

ILLUSION

1 part Cointreau
1 part Midori
1 part Vodka
1 part lemon juice
(shake)

I'M LONELY TONIGHT

1 part Bacardi
1 part Vodka
dash of Bitters
1 part lemon juice
ice
(build)

IRISH BANANA

1 part Banana Liqueur
1 part Baileys
1 part cream
½ a banana
ice
(blend)

ISLANDER

1 part Bacardi
1 part Malibu
1 part Banana Liqueur
(layer)

JAPANESE SLIPPER

1 part Cointreau
1 part Midori
1 part lemon juice
(shake)

JUMPING JACK

1 part Vodka
½ part Galliano
1 part lemon juice
top up with coke or lemonade
ice
(build)

JUNGLE JUICE

1 part Southern Comfort
1 part Bacardi
1 part Malibu
1 part cream
3 parts pineapple juice
½ a banana
ice
(blend)

KAMIKAZE

1 part Vodka
1 part Cointreau
½ part lemon juice
(dash of) lime cordial
ice
(build)

KRYPTONITE

1 part Blue Curacao
1 part Sambuca
6 parts pineapple juice
ice
(build)

LICK SIP SUCK

(always a fave)
1 nip Tequila
step 1: lick the salt
step 2: sip (scull) the Tequila
step 3: suck the lemon

LONG ISLAND ICED TEA

1 part Bacardi
1 part Vodka
1 part Tequila
1 part Gin
½ part Cointreau
½ part lemon juice
ice
(build in a tall glass)
top up with coke

LONG SLOW COMFORTABLE
SCREW UP AGAINST A WALL

1 part Southern Comfort
1 part Vodka
½ part Galliano
½ part Gin
4 parts orange juice
ice
(build)

MAI TAI

2 parts Bacardi
1 part Cointreau
1 part lime cordial
1 part lemon juice
dash of grenadine
(shake)

MANDINGO

1 part Midori
1 part Mango Liqueur
1 part lemon juice
tinned mango
ice
(blend)

MANGO MORNING

1 part Mango Liqueur
1 part Cointreau
tinned mango slices
1 part orange juice
1 part lemon juice
1 part sugar syrup
ice
(blend)

MARGUERITA

1 part Cointreau
1 part Tequila
1 part lemon juice
(shake)

FRUIT MARGUERITAS

make the Marguerita
then add:
Midori
or Strawberry Liqueur
or Mango Liqueur

add lots of ice
for a Frozen Marguerita
(blend)

MIDORI ALEXANDER

1 part Midori
1 part Creme de Cacao
2 parts cream
(shake)

MIND BENDER

1 part Tequila
1 part Banana Liqueur
1 part Blue Curacao
(layer)

MOIST SLIME

1 part Cointreau
½ part Galliano
½ part Creme de Menthe
2 parts pineapple juice
1 part cream
ice
(shake)

MOTHER

2 parts Baileys
1 part Malibu
1 part Vodka
dash of grenadine
ice
(blend)
use a champagne or martini glass

NICE ONE

1 part Malibu
1 part Banana Liqueur
1 part Vodka
3 parts pineapple juice
1 part cream
ice
(blend)

NOT NOW HONEY

1 part Kahlúa
1 part Strawberry Liqueur
1 part Brandy
strawberries
dash lemon juice
4 parts cream
grenadine
ice
(blend)

OPAL ORGASM

1 part cream
1 part Cointreau
1 part Baileys
1 part Opal Nera
(layer)

ORGASM

1 part Cointreau
1 part Baileys
(layer)

or (shake)
and pour over ice

ORGASM VARIATIONS

for a blended Orgasm
add milk and ice
(blend)

for a screaming one
add Galliano

for a multiple one
add Strawberry Liqueur

PINA COLADA

1 part Malibu
1 part Bacardi
3 parts pineapple juice
dash of cream
ice
(blend)

PINA COLADAS

(Fruit Coladas)
make the Pina Colada
then add 1 part Fruit Liqueur
and any fruit
try: Banana, or
Strawberry, or
Honeydew Melon

PINK SLIPPER

1 part Cointreau
1 part Bacardi
3 parts champagne
strawberries
ice
(blend)

PLASTERED POSSUM

1 part Midori
1 part Cointreau
1 part Galliano
4 parts pineapple juice
1 part cream
(shake)

1 part Baileys
1 part Midori
1 part Kahlúa
(layer)

QUICK ALEXANDER

1 part Midori
1 part Baileys
1 part Creme de Cacao
3 parts cream
(shake)

QUICK COMFORT

1 part Southern Comfort
1 part Midori
1 part Kahlúa
(layer)

SAFE SEX

1 part Cointreau
1 part Baileys
1 part Strawberry Liqueur
(layer)

SCUD MISSILE

1 part Malibu
1 part Baileys
1 part Kahlúa
    (layer)

SEX IN THE SNOW

1 part Cointreau
1 part Malibu
1 part Sambuca
(shot)

SEX ON THE BEACH

2 parts Midori
1 part Vodka
1 part Strawberry Liqueur
2 parts pineapple juice
dash of grenadine
ice
(blend)

SHORT LEG

1 part Cointreau
1 part Gin
2 parts orange juice
½ part lemon juice
ice
(build)

SLIPPERY NIPPLE

1 part Baileys
1 part Sambuca
(layer)

SLYDE YOUR THIGH

1 part Banana Liqueur
1 part Creme de Cacao
1 part Midori
2 parts cream
(shake)

SNAKE IN THE GRASS

2 parts Baileys
1 part Creme de Menthe
cream (optional)
(shake)

SPEARMINT SMOOTHIE

1 part Creme de Menthe
1 part Kahlúa
4 parts milk
2 parts cream
lots of ice
(blend)

SPLICE

1 part Midori
½ part Malibu
4 parts pineapple juice
1 part cream
ice
(blended)
add a dob of ice cream if you wish

STORMY MONDAY

1 part Southern Comfort
1 part Malibu
4 parts orange juice
ice
(build)

SWEET MARIA

1 part Bourbon
1 part Tia Maria
2 parts cream
(shake)

TEQUILA SUNRISE

1 part Tequila
8 parts orange juice
dash of grenadine (add last)
(build)

3-2-1

1 part Midori
1 part Strawberry Liqueur
1 part Banana Liqueur
(layer)

TIME OUT

1 part Brandy
1 part Kahlúa
2 parts orange juice
1 part cream
peaches
dash of grenadine
(blend)

2 B SLIPPERY

1 part Opal Nera
1 part lime cordial
ice
(build)

V-BOMB

2 parts Vodka
½ part lemon juice
add West Coast Cooler
ice
(build)
use a schooner glass

VELVET HUE

1 part Brandy
1 part Kahlúa
1 part Cointreau
3 parts cream
(shake)

VIBRATOR

1 part Baileys
1 part Malibu
1 part Banana Liqueur
(layer)

WHISPER

1 part Strawberry Liqueur
1 part Mango Liqueur
1 part lime juice
1 part lemon juice
peaches
ice
(blend)

ZOMBIE

1 part Bundy OP
1 part Bundy UP
1 part Bacardi
1 part Brandy
1 part sugar syrup
2 parts orange juice
2 parts pineapple juice
1 part lemon juice
ice
(shake)

ZULU WARRIOR

1 part Midori
1 part Strawberry Liqueur
1 part lemon juice
strawberries
rockmelon
ice
(blend)

THE PUNCH PAGE

Try these punches to add a little something to the evening, especially if there are going to be lots of people at the party *[Sangria's my favourite – Murray]*.

SANGRIA

1 bottle red wine (long flat red)
2 nips Brandy
2 nips Bacardi
2 nips Cointreau
orange juice (just refill wine bottle)
fruit (orange lemon apple)
sugar (to taste)
(1 nip = 30 ml)

TURTLE PUNCH

Green cordial
cask dry white wine
(test it in a glass before making the whole lot)

MIDORI PUNCH

1/2 a bottle Midori
1/2 a bottle Vodka
2 litre bottle lemonade
1 litre bottle pineapple juice
ice

GIN PUNCH

1 bottle Gin
1.25 litre pineapple juice
1.25 litre lemonade
3 nips lemon juice
1 litre orange juice
fruit

NON-ALCOHOLIC COCKTAILS

Just because someone has to drive, doesn't mean
they have to drink boring old Coke at the party,
make them something special. Call it a
"Joe Blow Special", or anything you like.
You may like to try one of the following drinks.
Bitters + orange juice + pineapple juice + ice
orange juice + lime cordial + lemon juice + ice
Shirley Temple = ginger ale + grenadine
Spider = Coke + ice cream

Blend various mixtures of fruit, ice and juices until you find
one you like.
Banana, strawberries, milk and ice blended is nice.
Mango and rockmelon blended with milk or juice
is also good.
Always put garnishes on non-alcoholic cocktails because
if you're sober, you want your drink to look nice, whereas
after you've had a few alcoholic ones, you tend not to care.
It is best to keep those people who have to drive, happy.

INDEX – BY NAME

INDEX – BY TYPE

INVITATION

To: _____

*We are having a legend cocktail party
and hope you can come*

Location: _____

_____

_____

Date: _____

Time: _____

Please bring: _____

_____

So get ready for some

LEGEND COCKTAILS

From: _____

_____

RSVP – Phone: _____

Date: _____